FREE TIME
ACTIVITIES

FOR AGES
7-9

MOLLY POTTER

A&C BLACK

Colossal thanks to...

**Chris Curtis for being the best and most bonkers playmate
anyone could ask for!**

Published 2008 by A & C Black Publishers Ltd
38 Soho Square, London W1D 3HB
www.acblack.com

ISBN 978-0-7136-8956-3

Written by Molly Potter
Design by Cathy Tincknell
Illustration by Mike Phillips

Copyright © Molly Potter 2008

Printed in Great Britain by Martins the Printers, Berwick-on- Tweed

This book is produced using paper that is made from wood grown in managed, sustainable forests. It
is natural, renewable and recyclable. The logging and manufacturing processes conform to the
environmental regulations of the country of origin.

To see our full range of books visit
www.acblack.com

CONTENTS

INTRODUCTION

WHY WOULD YOU USE THIS BOOK?

It can be exhausting perpetually inventing new ideas to keep children purposefully and happily occupied – a task many teachers, club leaders and teaching assistants are faced with every day. *Free Time Activities* provides ready-made, interesting, varied and quirky ideas that can be used with individuals or groups of children in many different settings e.g.

• Breakfast clubs
• After school clubs
• Any children's club
• Last minute cover for a class or group of children
• For end of term fun
• During wet breaks
• As golden time or a treat for an individual pupil or group of pupils

Each activity has clear instructions and those designed for individual work require minimal teacher intervention.Children will be inspired and entertained by the activities in this book and motivation to do them should not be an issue. Most of the activities require little more than a pencil and a vivid imagination!

> *Imagination is more important than knowledge...*
> ALBERT EINSTEIN US (GERMAN-BORN) PHYSICIST (1879 - 1955)

HOW IS THE BOOK ORGANISED?

The activities in this book are split into three sections.
Section 1: Activities best completed by individual children
Section 2: Activities suited to pairs or small groups of children
Section 3: Activities for a group of children, ideally led by an adult

Equipment is deliberately kept to a minimum and a list of what's needed for each activity is provided on the contents page. Most of the activities in the first two sections simply require a photocopy of the activity and then a pencil, coloured pens and, in some instances, extra paper. The activities that are led by an adult (in the third section) for the most part can be done by reading directly from the book, although sometimes a photocopy of the page is essential to help pupils complete the task. With these particular activities we recommend that the supervising adult selects an activity and prepares any equipment that might be needed in advance.

HOW COULD THE ACTIVITIES BE EXTENDED AND PRESENTED?

Most of the ideas could be extended in one way or another and need not end with the task that is laid out on the page. On some pages there are specific suggestions listed under 'More to do!' but here are some generic examples of how this can be done, although not all of these examples will be suitable for all activities.

CHILDREN COULD:

- Make their own version of the activity, or they could alter or add some ideas to the existing one.
- Devise their own extension activity, present it to the class or group, and then vote on the one they all would like to do.
- Explain to another child what they did – perhaps without using words!
- Add to or colour in any picture or turn it into a collage.
- Give each other positive feedback on how well the task was completed.
- Work out a way of evaluating or ranking the activities for enjoyment, difficulty, humour, etc.
- Vote for any activity or part of an activity they might like to do or see again (particularly relevant to drama activities).
- Produce a letter, postcard, interview, advert, radio advert, newspaper report, poster, quiz, memory test, puzzle, fact bubbles, time-line, labelled diagrams, questionnaire, list, map, cartoon, graph to do with the activity.

YOU COULD:

- Make a display of any ideas that were produced from the activities.
- Create a book of the ideas, pictures or materials the children have produced.
- Photograph or video some of the activities for a classroom display or to show to other classes or assemblies.
- Use one of the activities, especially the drama ones, as the focus for a class assembly.

GUESS DESIGN COPY

DRAW IMAGINE

CONSIDER MAKE UP ACT CUT

EXPLAIN DISCUSS BALANCE ADJUST

LAUGH

PRETEND DEVELOP

QUESTION PICTURE THINK

MIME SORT WONDER

COLOUR PLAN DESCRIBE

IMPROVE PONDER ILLUSTRATE

HAPPY OR ANGRY?

It's easy to tell if a person is happy or angry by their body language. It's also easy to tell if a Grik is happy or angry because it shows it in the same way as people do. The other creatures here show their moods in different ways, e.g. a Haggit might show it's angry by firing wax balls from its ears. Think of different ways in which the Haggit, Floomp and Tartil might show they are happy or angry and draw them in the boxes below.

Creature	When it feels nothing!	Happy	Angry
Grik			
Haggit			
Floomp			
Tartil			

THE NURSERY RHYME TIMES

Here are some *shocking* headlines about well-known nursery rhymes.
Draw a picture to go with each story.

LITTLE MISS MUFFET'S SPIDER WAS, IN FACT, A RABBIT!

Miss Muffet says, "Of course I'm not scared of a fluffy little bunny. Had I known, I would have happily continued to eat my curds and whey. I have seen so many spiders hanging around that spot before that when I caught something out of the corner of my eye – I just assumed it was a spider."

LITTLE BO PEEP DIDN'T LOSE A SINGLE SHEEP!

In a court case, Little Bo Peep stood her ground and said she had a foolproof system that meant she knew exactly where every single sheep was at any point in time. She went on to say that she would never be so careless as to let them just wander home by themselves.

THREE BLIND MICE SAY PUNISHMENT WAS UNFAIR.

The removal of their tails with a carving knife was considered to be too harsh. One blind mouse said, "We thought the farmer's wife would find it funny – we didn't mean to scare her." Two of the mice had a tail replacement operation but the third is waiting for the farmer's wife to pay compensation.

THE KING'S MEN COULD HAVE PUT HUMPTY TOGETHER AGAIN!

Shocking news uncovered as one of the king's men reveals they could have in fact mended Humpty but had felt, at the time, they had more pressing priorities. These pressing priorities turned out to be a game of golf!

MORE TO DO!

Design a new front page for the *Nursery Rhyme Times* with a shocking headline about one of the following nursery rhymes (or you could use a well-known fairy tale).

- HEY, DIDDLE, DIDDLE
- THE GRAND OLD DUKE OF YORK
- BAA, BAA, BLACK SHEEP
- JACK AND JILL
- TWINKLE, TWINKLE, LITTLE STAR
- OLD MOTHER HUBBARD
- SING A SONG OF SIXPENCE
- THIS LITTLE PIGGY WENT TO MARKET

Free Time Activities 7-9 © Molly Potter 2008

WEIRD AND WONDERFUL

Turn all these shapes into pictures of different things e.g. monsters,
aliens, weird plants or anything else you can think of!
Make sure you use all of each shape.

DONKIT AND GOPHANT RIDING

The Donkit and Gophant are two creatures found in Cachak. Both are used for riding in the same way as we might use horses. Unfortunately, both creatures move in an extremely bouncy way and even the most skilful riders often end up falling off.

You have been sent to Cachak to design a saddle and a bridle for these two creatures. Think about your design by looking carefully at the pictures below. Now draw a picture of someone riding a Donkit and a Gophant using the saddle and bridle you have designed. You can use the illustrations at the bottom of the page or start your drawing from scratch.

A Donkit

Strong spikes that wobble a lot – the Donkit refuses to move if its spikes are not free to wobble.

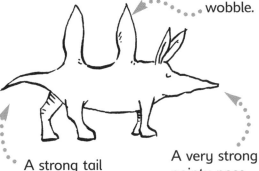

A strong tail

A very strong pointy nose

A Gophant

Strong ears

A flat back

A boney chin

A very strong tail

9

ALIEN CRIME

The crime of 'dagar splatting' has been committed by an alien. A sketch of the alien has been created using the description given by a witness to the crime.

Unfortunately, the witness is not happy with the sketch and corrections need to be made. Can you re-draw the sketch by reading what the witness said?

1. The chin was more pointed.

2. It had four eyes that got slightly bigger from left to right.

3. Its eyebrows were much thicker.

4. The two outside teeth pointed upwards, above the mouth, while the middle two were as shown in the sketch.

5. The spot was on the left side of its nose, not the right.

6. Its ears were not pointed – they were big and round and stuck out a lot.

7. Its hair was a really curly blob on top of its head.

8. It had seven antennae, not two.

NEW CONSTELLATIONS

Many years ago, people looked at the stars and saw pictures in them. Each picture that they made with a group of stars was called a 'constellation'. Here are two well-known constellations.

Leo, the lion

Aquarius, the water carrier

Use the dots below to make four constellations of your own and then give each one a name.

Free Time Activities 7-9 © Molly Potter 2008

CRAZY CRIMINALS

Complete these wanted posters. All the criminals have committed crazy crimes!

WANTED

BULGY-EYED BOB
WANTED FOR: PAINTING ALL THE
LINES ON THE ROAD GREY
REWARD: FREE PARKING FOR LIFE

WANTED

HORRIBLY-HAIRY HORACE
WANTED FOR: POPPING EVERY
CRISP PACKET IN TOWN
REWARD:

WANTED

WARTY WYLIE
WANTED FOR:

REWARD:

WANTED

WANTED FOR:

REWARD:

Free Time Activities 7-9 © Molly Potter 2008

LABEL PERSON!

Draw a person to match the labels. Follow the numbers in the correct order as this will make it easier to draw. Add anything else you think is needed to finish the drawing and colour it in.

(13) Spiky hair

(9) Small eyes, close together

(10) Thick dark eyebrows

(11) Rosy cheeks

(12) Big round ears

(6) Big round nose

(7) Big smile

(8) Two teeth that stick out

(1) Long thin arms

(2) Little shorts

(4) Round knees

(3) Long thin legs

(5) Big feet

Answer on p62

Free Time Activities 7-9 © Molly Potter 2008

STAMPS, FLAGS AND COINS

In the table below are details of three different imaginary countries, Dolopia, Zakan and Bozil. You have been asked to design a stamp, a flag and a coin for each country. To do this you will need to use the information in the table below and to imagine what you think some of the things might look like.

	DOLOPIA	ZAKAN	BOZIL
HEAD OF STATE	King Large Nose	Queen Long Neck	President Huge Ears
WEATHER	Gusts of wind and snow	Sun, rain and rainbows	Lots of thunder storms
LANDSCAPE	Lots of mountains with different shaped tops	Lots of lakes, rivers and colourful trees	Completely flat with round rocks here and there
NATIONAL PASTIME	Playing Truffball	Zaroose spotting	Grar racing
MOST COMMON ANIMAL	Flat-headed Grogilla	Bushy-tailed Floog	Big-footed Plapper

DOLOPIA

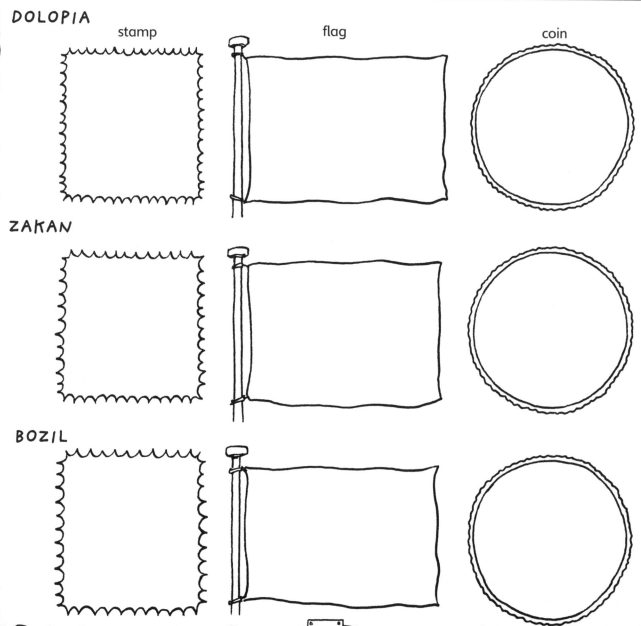

stamp   flag   coin

ZAKAN

BOZIL

SASOOP'S SHOP

This is Sasoop Watson. He is a Snartz. He owns a shop and he stocks all the things a Snartz needs to remain happy.

Here is just one shelf in his shop with the following items for sale:

•SUPER SPIKE HAIR CREAM — for the perfect Snartz spikes

•COLOUR-CHANGE WASHING POWDER — all clothes come out the washing machine a different colour with every wash

•CANNED SPLY NUTS — a Snartz' favourite snack

•SPARKLY CLAWS — claws for that special night out

•FLAZZLEPOP — (a Snartz favourite) — a drink that comes in many different flavours and temperatures

•PUTTAPATTERN — a pattern that can be squirted on clothing and shoes.

Decide which container is holding which product and design a label for each one. Either use the names given or make up some of your own.

Free Time Activities 7-9 © Molly Potter 2008

ALIENS' UNIFORM

On Spaceship Krik 5000 some new jobs have recently been given to four aliens. It has been decided that these four aliens need uniforms to suit their work and you have been asked to design them. Draw your designs on this sheet.

Spaceship driver

Map reader (navigator)

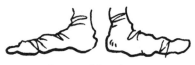

Spaceship cleaner

Chef

FEEDING HAGRUFF

This is Hagruff.

Hagruff is from the land of Leydenia where the food is a little different from the stuff we know. Can you make up some more examples of the food Hagruff eats and draw the pictures to go with them?

FOOD NAME	DESCRIPTION	PICTURE
Frigizz	A red slime with green triangles in it. It tastes a bit like tomato ketchup mixed with sherbet.	
Yallow	Yellow balls (about 10cm across) that feel like marshmallows but taste like mud and vinegar.	
Bloop		

Free Time Activities 7-9 © Molly Potter 2008

A FOUR SEASONS CLOCK

A clock factory has decided to make a clock that has a single hand that goes round once a year. It has been decided that the clock will be decorated to show the differences between the seasons. You have been asked to design it. Think of all the things you can use to decorate each part of the clock. Here are some ideas:

WINTER
COLOURS: grey, white, black
THEMES: trees with no leaves, snow men, snow ball fights, ice, snowdrops, hibernating hedgehogs, winter clothes

SPRING
COLOURS: yellow, pink, light green, white
THEMES: blossom, daffodils, bunnies, April showers, bluebells

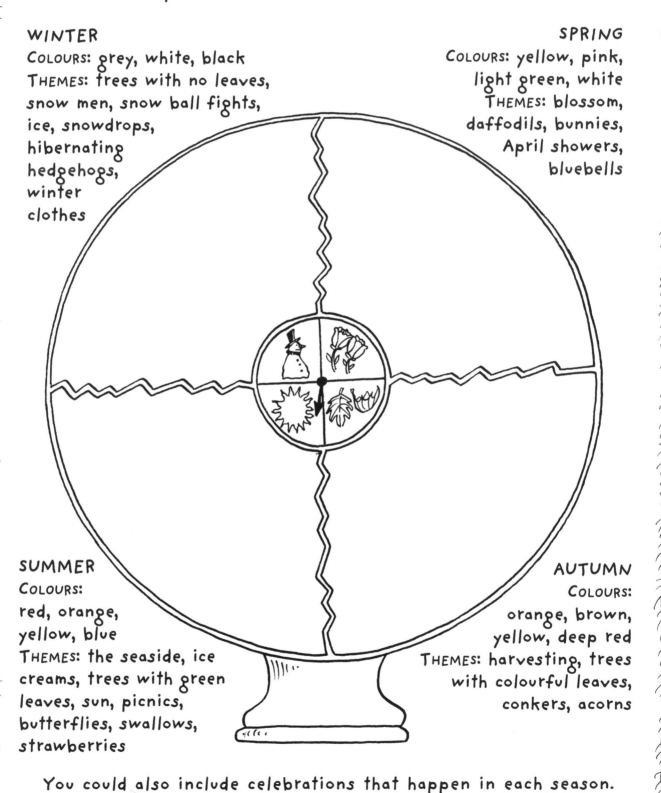

SUMMER
COLOURS: red, orange, yellow, blue
THEMES: the seaside, ice creams, trees with green leaves, sun, picnics, butterflies, swallows, strawberries

AUTUMN
COLOURS: orange, brown, yellow, deep red
THEMES: harvesting, trees with colourful leaves, conkers, acorns

You could also include celebrations that happen in each season.

AN INTERGALACTIC BEAUTY CONTEST

Draw the two missing contestants in the final of the intergalactic beauty contest.

RAGUMP

ZARGOOL

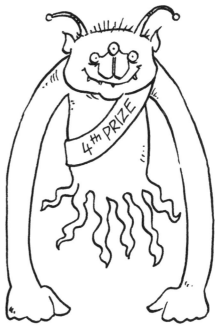

MR GALAXY 3.6

TRAFFY

DESIGN A SHOP SIGN

Design an eye-catching sign for the following shops:

A lighting shop called DEE LIGHTS

A pet shop called MOLLYCODDLES.

A luxury food store called DELI — SSH.

A shop that sells magic called SPELLS.

ALIEN CREEPY CRAWLIES

On Planet Zippo there are lots of different kinds of creepy crawlies.
Many of them are related to those we have on earth

This is a Butterspike
and it is related to
the Butterfly...

...and this is a
Ratterfippar which
is related to the
Caterpillar.

This is the leaf of a Razip tree that is found on Planet Zippo.
Insects love to eat these leaves. Draw the alien creepy crawlies on
this leaf that are related to:

- the snail
- the centipede
- the ant
- the moth
- the spider
- the ladybird
- the worm
- the bee
- the dragonfly
- the slug
- the fly

Free Time Activities 7-9 © Molly Potter 2008

A VARRAMENIAN BEACH

You are on holiday in the imaginary land of Varramenia and you are going to send a postcard to a friend. You are on a Varramenian beach but it is nothing like the ones back home because you can eat anything on the beach. The sand is sparkly, the sea is frothy and the pebbles are many different colours and everything has a different flavour.

Draw a picture of a Varramenian beach on the front of your postcard.

Make up an address for your friend and then tell them about your beach holiday.

THE DEMANDS OF FLORRIE

Meet Florrie. She is a superstar where she comes from. This portrait was made of her. Because Florrie is so vain, she says that more needs to be added to it to make her look stunning, before anyone else is allowed to see it. Follow Florrie's instructions below to try and make her happier about the portrait.

I want...

the spikes of my hair to all be different colours

blue eye shadow – darker at the edges and lighter in the middle

the spot on my cheek turned into a star shape

huge colourful earrings that are an interesting shape

bright red lipstick

my T-shirt to have my name on it – and I need it to be purple

a pretty necklace

the same bracelet on each wrist, pretty ones of course, with spiral patterns on them.

a really complicated and colourful pattern on my shorts, with no white spaces.

my toe nails painted a bright colour.

a colourful ankle bracelet.

Free Time Activities 7-9 © Molly Potter 2008

SNARGILL AT LARGE!

This sign warns of a big-footed Snargill on the loose!

This is a picture of one.

SIGN

PICTURE

Make up names for the creatures on these warning signs and draw the pictures to go with them.

NAME_____

PICTURE

NAME_____

PICTURE

NAME_____

PICTURE

CAMP SITE

When Class X4 of Zargoo Primary School went on a camping trip, the teachers had a very tricky time putting them in tents so that they were all happy. However, they managed it in the end. Using the notes and pictures below can you work out how this was done? Put the names of the occupants beside each tent.

Boys	Narp Tooly Flar Simp Baz Pluff Timp Toop
Girls	Gizz Plippy Kaz Daff Moop

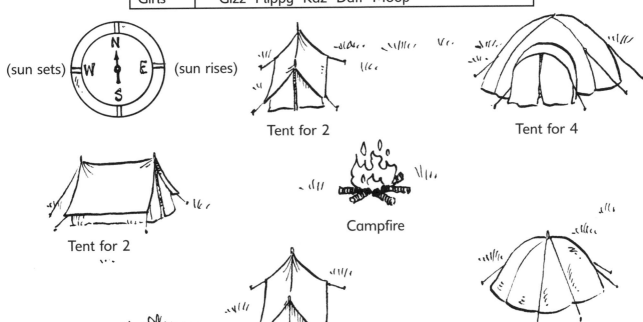

(sun sets) W — E (sun rises)

Tent for 2

Tent for 4

Tent for 2

Campfire

Tent for 2

Tent for 3

NOTES
1. Males and females must not be in the same tent
2. Boys were in the tent for 4
3. Females were in the tent for 3
4. Plippy insisted on being with Kaz only
5. Narp insisted on being in a tent that had its door opposite Plippy's
6. Baz and Toop insisted on being together on their own
7. Pluff refused to be in a tent with more than one other person
8. Baz wanted to have his tent's door positioned so he could watch the sun rise from his sleeping bag
9. Pluff's tent was next to the boys' tent for four

MORE TO DO!
Draw a picture of the creatures posing for a photo behind the campfire.

Answer on p62

Free Time Activities 7-9 © Molly Potter 2008

LITTLE EMERGENCIES

Some people find mornings ever so difficult! Bob Patterson has a solution. He drives a 'morning emergency vehicle' that will arrive at your house in the morning and deal with any little emergencies you might have. The kind of emergencies he has dealt with this week are:

- Having no milk for cereal
- A button falling off an outfit
- Messy hair
- Broken shoe laces
- Clothes still damp from washing
- Running out of toothpaste
- Only being able to find one shoe
- Alarm clock not going off – lateness!
- Losing keys

When people ring his number 101, he drives his emergency vehicle straight round and deals with whatever is the problem.

1. Can you think of any more emergencies that he might have to deal with?

2. Have a go at drawing his morning emergency vehicle. Label all the parts of his vehicle that are useful when he comes to the rescue, e.g. he might have a milk tank or a really strong magnet to find keys.

3. Have a go at drawing his uniform!

MORE TO DO!

Think of other little emergencies people might have and what the vehicle that comes to the rescue would look like. Here are some ideas to get you started.

Little emergencies at:
- Children's parties
- In a supermarket
- In a lesson or assembly at school
- In a park
- In a friendship

DESIGN A TROPHY

Here are two trophies that were awarded to...

THE WORLD'S GREATEST
LOVER OF MATHS.

THE WORLD'S BEST
BIG HEAD.

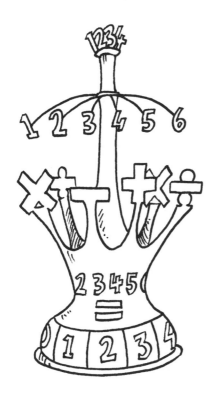

Can you design trophies for the following:
- The world's best shopper
- The world's best animal lover
- The world's most colourful person
- The world's tidiest person
- The world's messiest person
- The world's best friend
- The world's most clumsy person
- The world's best teacher's pet
- The world's nosiest person
- The world's most excited person
- The world's best mistake maker
- The world's safest person
- The world's deepest sleeper

MORE TO DO!
Think of your own award and design the trophy for it.

Free Time Activities 7-9 © Molly Potter 2008

A FAIRGROUND WITH A DIFFERENCE

This is a rather unusual fairground with many strange rides. Very close to the entrance (just to the left of this picture) there is a stall that serves food. It is, of course, also rather unusual.

Draw what you think the food stall looks like. Let your imagination go wild and make the actual stall, the food, any seats for people, the way of paying, straws, plates, etc, extremely bizarre! Remember that in most ordinary fairs things like hotdogs, candyfloss, toffee apples, chips, burgers and drinks are on sale.

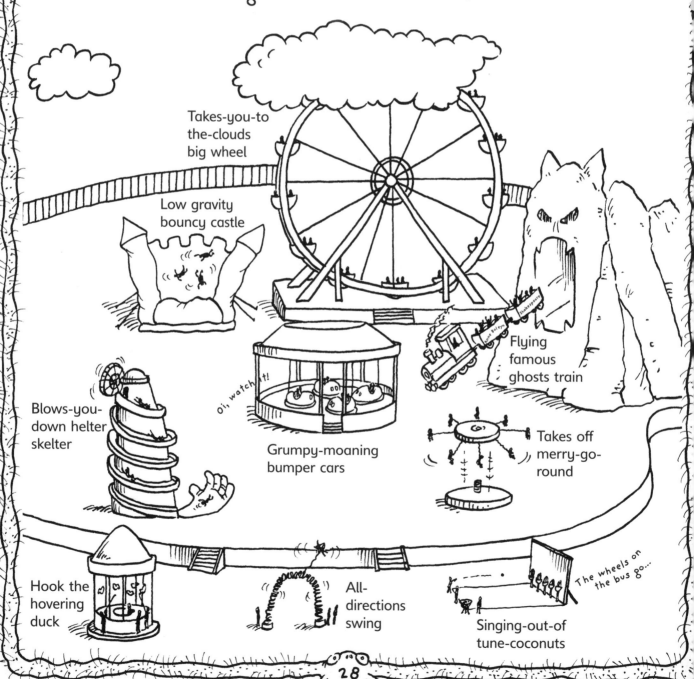

Takes-you-to the-clouds big wheel

Low gravity bouncy castle

Flying famous ghosts train

Oi, watch it!

Blows-you-down helter skelter

Grumpy-moaning bumper cars

Takes off merry-go-round

Hook the hovering duck

All-directions swing

Singing-out-of tune-coconuts

The wheels on the bus go...

THIS IS BLINTY

Blinty has a girlfriend. His girlfriend could not look more different from him. In other words, while Blinty is thin, his girlfriend is fat. Blinty has a large round nose, while his girlfriend's nose is small and pointy. Imagine what Blinty's girlfriend might look like and draw a picture of her. See if anyone else's picture looks anything like yours!

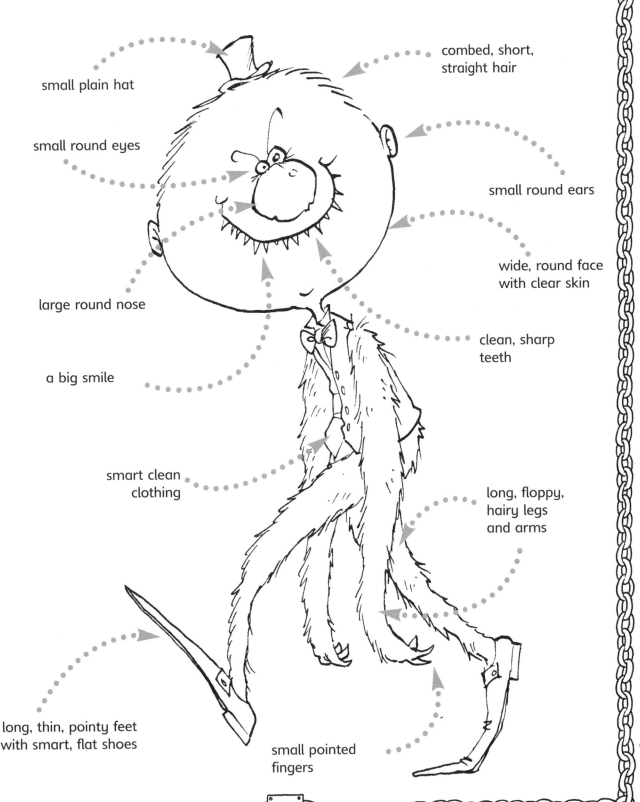

small plain hat

combed, short, straight hair

small round eyes

small round ears

large round nose

wide, round face with clear skin

a big smile

clean, sharp teeth

smart clean clothing

long, floppy, hairy legs and arms

long, thin, pointy feet with smart, flat shoes

small pointed fingers

THE DANGERS OF FAIRY TALE LAND

This is Fairy tale land and it is not a very safe place to be! Draw the warning signs that need to be positioned in the places marked on the map e.g. the 'danger' near Cinderella's house is being bossed around by two ugly sisters. Think about the 'dangers' that could be found in the different places and draw a sign to warn people. There might be more than one 'danger' in some places.

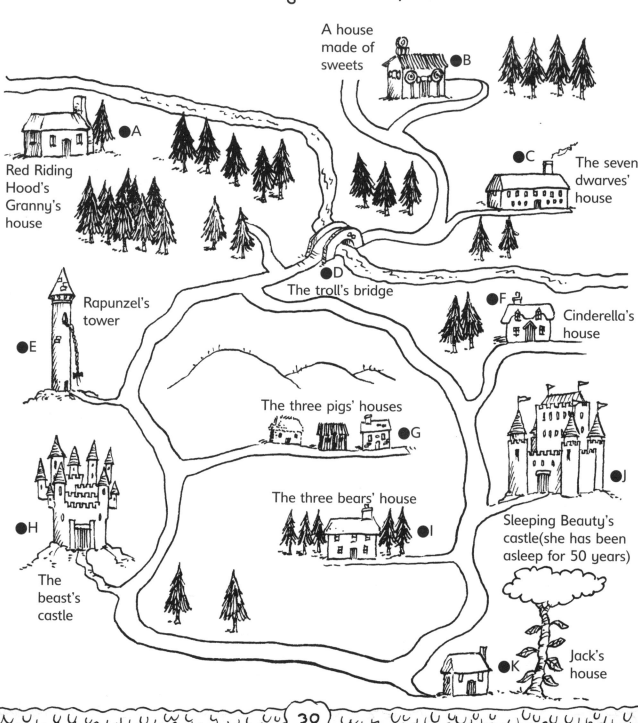

A house made of sweets — B

Red Riding Hood's Granny's house — A

The seven dwarves' house — C

The troll's bridge — D

Rapunzel's tower — E

Cinderella's house — F

The three pigs' houses — G

The beast's castle — H

The three bears' house — I

Sleeping Beauty's castle (she has been asleep for 50 years) — J

Jack's house — K

CLOWNS

On a separate piece of paper draw a picture of a clown by choosing one thing from each of these boxes and putting them together.

Noses

Eyes

Hair

Mouths

Hats

Necks

Bodies

Things clowns use

Free Time Activities 7-9 © Molly Potter 2008

MOPPACO FASHION WEEK

Each year, the creatures of Moppaco spend a week celebrating fashion. Every creature has an outfit designed especially for them which they show off on the catwalk. These four creatures are panicking because they haven't managed to find anyone to design their outfits. They have asked you to have a go!

FLOOF

Floof likes his clothes to fit tightly. He loves colourful buttons and zigzag patterns. He also likes hats that show off his tufty ears.

THIGOR

Thigor likes clothing that has tassels and frills. He quite likes his outfits to make him look bigger than he is. He also likes zips.

BELLOMP

Bellomp likes clothing that shows off his tiny waist. He is a fan of really fancy gloves with matching hats.

POL

Pol loves anything that he can get into because his shape is so awkward to dress. However, he does like long, curly shoes.

BIZARRE OLYMPICS

At the Bizarre Olympics people are forging tickets so that they can get in to see the events. Because of this, a team have been brought in to change the ticket design for each event every day. This was yesterday's ticket for the cloud skiing event.

You are part of this team and these are the tickets you need to design today.
- Dolphin water polo
- Synchronised rowing (with bubble bath in the water)
- Low gravity gymnastics
- Obstacle course skating
- Chuck the huge foam ball
- Running races on jelly
- Feather fighting
- Trampolining with a ball
- Elephant lifting

Remember that you need the tickets to be detailed and in colour so they are difficult to copy quickly.

MORE TO DO!
Can you think of any other events that might happen at the Bizarre Olympics?

Think about all the sports that happen in the Olympics: running, javelin, cycling, wrestling, swimming, diving, jumping (high and long), hurdles, archery, football, ice hockey, marathons, relay, judo, fencing, badminton, boxing, horse jumping, sailing, tennis, shooting, etc, and use these sports to help you.

Free Time Activities 7-9 © Molly Potter 2008

MONSTER BATH TIME

Here are three different monsters having a bath. Draw a picture of what you think they look like when they are out of the bath (with their trunks/swimming costumes on!).

Free Time Activities 7-9 © Molly Potter 2008

FLIPLAND LAWS

In the imaginary country of Flipland there are lots of laws that people visiting the cities and towns have to obey. Some of the laws might seem a little odd to you or me, but the people of Flipland have to abide by them or they end up being fined. Unfortunately, everyone finds it quite hard to remember all the laws so to remind them, the country has a sign maker that paints little signs. The sign maker tries to keep his signs very simple and rarely uses words. Here is an example of one of his signs.

THE LAW
All shopping lists must be written neatly.

THE SIGN

See if you can draw a suitable sign for the following laws.

- If you walk your dog in the town, it must wear slippers.
- You must smile, wave and nod at everyone you meet.
- 'Thank you' and 'please' always to be said very loudly.
- Hats must be worn between noon and 2 p.m.
- No tutting or putting hands on hips at any time.
- Only apples or bananas can be eaten outside.
- Everyone over 12 must do a funny walk when they cross the road, to entertain children.
- Pushchairs are only allowed in the special lanes provided.
- Bicycles need to have balloons attached to them to make them easy to see.
- People are only allowed to stand still in the circles especially painted on the ground for this reason.
- Benches are only for children under 6 and people over 70 years of age.
- All litter to be folded neatly before it is placed in the bin.
- People trying to get into a shop must give way to people coming out of the shop.

MORE TO DO!
- Make up some new laws and draw the signs for them.
- Have a go at drawing a picture of a street in Flipland!

ALIEN WASHING LINE

Here is a black and white photo of a washing line from Planet Tyra. It is the washing from one alien family. It is not known how many aliens are in the family but it is known that no two aliens look the same.

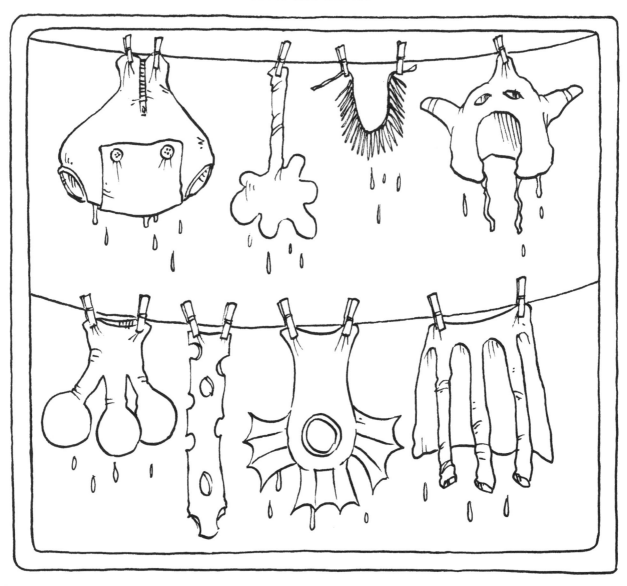

Imagine the members of the alien family that wear these clothes and draw a picture of the family wearing them. You might draw a family of eight with each member wearing one of the items, or you might like to draw fewer aliens and have some of them wearing two or even three items of clothing.

Remember, we do not know what colour the clothing is or which part/s of the body the alien wears it on! You will have to make it all up! The clothing might be worn like humans wear the following: hat, scarf, socks, gloves, dress, skirt, balaclava, top, trousers or it might be something that an alien wears on a body part humans just don't have!

Free Time Activities 7-9 © Molly Potter 2008

INDOOR SCAVENGER HUNT

See how many of the following items you can find. When you find one, either draw a small picture of it or describe where you found it. Try not to use the same thing twice.

Something that is a triangle shape	Something that could fit inside a matchbox	A person's name written down	Something that bends that is NOT paper
A strand of hair that you can stick in this box	A letter 'J'	Something you found on the floor that you can pick up and stick in this box	Something that is only one colour
Something that makes a high note when you tap it	Something that folds	Something that will make a smudge in this box	Something that smells
A circle	Something red	A capital letter 'A'	A liquid
A picture or a photo of a person	A straight line that is longer than 5cm but shorter than 10cm	Something with a curved edge	A sign that asks you to do something

Free Time Activities 7-9 © Molly Potter 2008

STAIN PICTURE

This is Ralph. At the moment his hair is white, but he would love it to be multi-coloured. He has asked you to stain his hair as many different colours as you can but without using felt pens, pencils, crayons or paints!

FUNNY SUMS

Work with a friend.
Here are two 'word sums' that have been done for you.

SNOWMAN + HAIRDRYER = A PUDDLE

MESSY HAIR + COMB = LOUD SCREAMING

Can you suggest what the answers to these 'word sums' might be?
Draw or write your answer. Of course the answer can't be wrong!

TODDLER + CHOCOLATE SAUCE =

TENT — PEGS =

CAKE $\div$ FRIENDS =

TREE X 1000 =

TEABAGS + SCISSORS + CHIMPANZEE =

PERSON — GLASSES =

BOUNCY CASTLE + FIZZY DRINKS =

TIE + GRAVY =

HICCUPS + PAINTING A LINE IN THE MIDDLE OF THE ROAD =

COW + TRAMPOLINE =

BUSY STREET + £2 COIN ON THE FLOOR =

_____ + _____ = A HUGE MESS

MORE TO DO!
Make up some 'word sums' of your own for other people to do.

Free Time Activities 7-9 © Molly Potter 2008

TEST YOUR 'OTHER' HAND

Work with a friend and compare how you get on! If you are right-handed, this is about testing your left hand and if you are left- handed this is about testing your right hand. Use your 'other' hand to try and do the following.

1. Join up these dots as neatly as you can.

2. Write the name of an animal as neatly as you can so that someone can read it.

_____

3. Draw a friend so that someone can guess who you have drawn!

4. Draw a line between these two dots without going outside the border.

5. Join up all the numbers in this box without touching one of the lines.

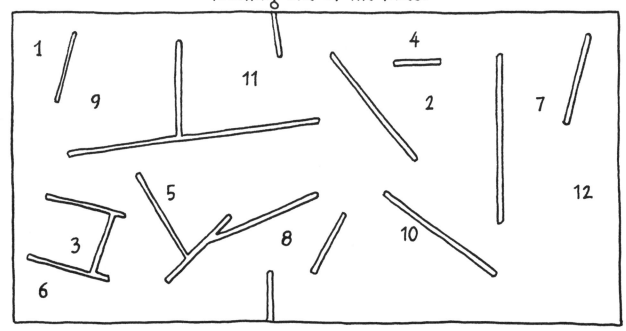

6. Draw a spiral on the back of this sheet, with the lines as close as you can get them but without any lines crossing.

MORE 'TO DO!

Make up some tests of your own to try on your friends.

HIDE THE NUMBERS

In this picture of a crowd, see if you can hide each of the numbers from 0 to 9 (they can be any way up). Hide your numbers in the lines of the picture or add extra parts to hide them in. You could even add patterns to clothing. Hide the numbers so a person would have to look quite carefully to find them.

MORE TO DO!

Draw a picture of one of the following and hide the numbers 0-9 in it. See if a friend can find all the numbers!
- A picture of flowers, trees, plant and insects
- Children playing with sports equipment in a playground
- A person in a shed full of DIY tools and garden equipment

CREATURE FACTS

Work with a friend and use both your imaginations to make up lots of details about both of these creatures.

Name:

Height:

Colour/s:

Sound it makes:

Food it eats:

Where it lives:

What it likes:

What it doesn't like:

Is it dangerous? YES/NO
If YES, in what way:

What it can do (e.g. wag its tails):

Colour/s:

Sound it makes:

Food it eats:

Where it lives:

What it likes:

What it doesn't like:
Is it dangerous? YES/NO
If YES, in what way:

What it can do (e.g. swim across the Atlantic):

Name:

Height:

WEIRD WORD HUNT!

How many three letter words can you find in this word hunt? All you need to do is draw a straight line through three letters that make a word (without any other letters getting in the way). One has been done for you, to make the word 'mop'. Use a ruler to help you. The words all go consonant — vowel — consonant and can be read in any direction.

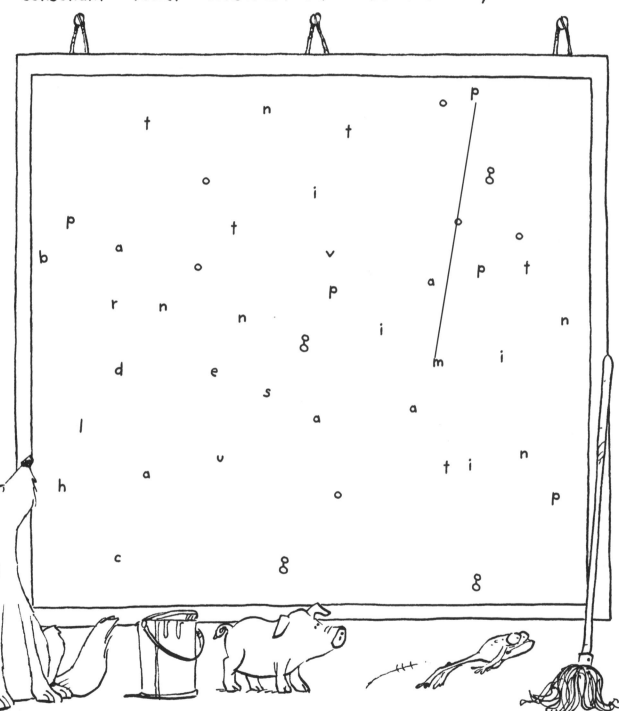

MORE TO DO!

Make a word hunt like this one for a friend to do. You will probably need a ruler and a rubber to help you do this.

Answer on p63

43

Free Time Activities 7–9 © Molly Potter 2008

WHAT WOULD IT LOOK LIKE?

Work with a friend and talk about or draw your ideas.

1. What would an umbrella look like if rain was made of £5 notes?

2. What would a door knocker for a deaf person look like?

3. What would a fork look like if all food was magnetic?

4. What would a hat look like if our head had a large point on top of it?

5. What would spectacles look like if we had two noses and one ear?

6. What would a glue spreader look like if glue was like sand?

7. What would a purse look like if all coins had a hole in the middle for carrying purposes?

8. What would a shoe look like if our feet were like cubes stuck on the end of our leg?

9. What would a wheelbarrow look like if it was made to carry things up a very steep slope?

10. What would an apple look like if it could be peeled using just your hands?

THE MINISTRY OF CHANGE

The Ministry of Change is an organisation that makes changes to stop people from becoming bored. Here are some examples of the kind of changes the ministry has made in the past:

- Made everyone eat dessert before their main course
- Painted all roadside paths purple with green kerbs
- Made sitting in lifts compulsory
- Given all post boxes a flashing light on top that flashed for a minute after a letter was posted
- Changed traffic lights so that they shouted their commands as well as having arms that gave directions
- Made clocks go 'bip bop' instead of 'tick tock'
- Got people to lend books to libraries

You have been asked to attend the latest meeting at the Ministry and they would like to hear your suggestions on how the following might be changed. Work with a partner to come up with as many suggestions for changes as you can:

1. Shaking hands to greet people
2. Putting candles that are the age a person has reached on top of birthday cakes
3. Clapping to show your appreciation at the end of a performance
4. Talking about the weather when you meet people you don't know in the street
5. Men and boys wearing a tie when they wish to dress smartly for something
6. Wrapping up presents before you give them to someone
7. Nodding your head for 'yes' and shaking your head for 'no'
8. Tutting to show you don't like something
9. Putting your hand up in lessons to show you think you know the answer

Free Time Activities 7-9 © Molly Potter 2008

PLANET ZOOG

| zig | zag | zoot | zog | zax | zaz |

On the planet Zoog, children do not have a mother and a father, they just have two 'parents'. As on Earth, you can often see who a child's parents are because the child looks similar in some ways to their parents. Which two creatures (above) do you think are the parents of the children below?

 Parents are:

_____ & _____

 Parents are:

_____ & _____

Parents are:

_____ & _____

Parents are:

_____ & _____

 Parents are:

_____ & _____

Parents are:

_____ & _____

Now draw creature that could be the child of the following parents.

1. ZIG and ZAG
2. ZOOT and ZOG
3. ZAX and ZAZ
4. ZIG AND ZAZ
5. ZOG and ZAX
6. ZOOT and ZAG
7. ZIG and ZOOT
8. ZAZ and ZOG

MORE TO DO!

Make up some of your own creatures and their children. See if someone else can guess which creatures are related to which parents.

Answer on p63

Free Time Activities 7-9 © Molly Potter 2008

THE LONGEST LIST...

Work with a friend and try and create the longest list you can for each of the following things:

- Things that could fit in a matchbox.

- Things that can be bigger than an elephant.

- Things that car drivers in this country have to do when they are on the road so that they do not break the law.

- Nursery rhymes that have animals or a creature in them.

- Noises that animals make.

- Yellow foods.

- Festivals or celebrations that happen on the same date each year.

- Words that mean 'big' and words that mean 'small'.

- Ways of preparing or cooking eggs.

- Things that can be cut with scissors.

- Liquids other than water.

- Sports that use a ball.

- Things than run on electricity.

- Things that can only be made of metal.

- Letters and numbers that are also words or names (including two or more together than might make a word) e.g. B4 (before) or NRG (energy).

Examples on p64

HARD TO COPY

Can you put patterns, colours and shapes on to this £10 note to make it hard to copy? When you have finished, see if a friend can copy it!

Your £10 note.

£10

A copy of it by your friend.

£10

WHERE'S THE SPIDER?

Can you fill this picture with leaves, grasses, insects and flowers and then hide a spider (like the one below) so it would be hard to find? See if your friend can find the spider.

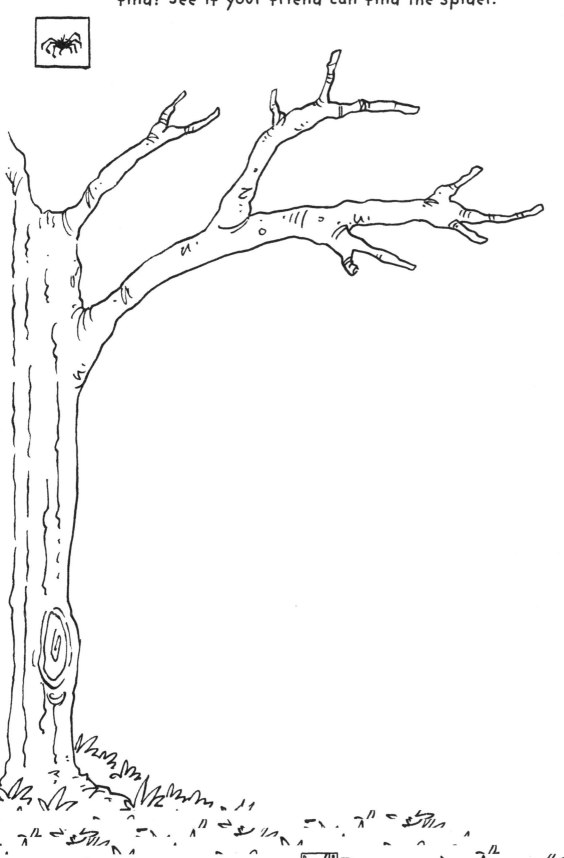

Free Time Activities 7-9 © Molly Potter 2008

CONVEYOR BELT PUDDINGS

In Gertrude's Spectacular Pudding Restaurant, you can eat just about any pudding you can think of. All the puddings are made by a pudding machine with a control panel. Different buttons are pressed to make the combination of bases, sauces and toppings that people ask for. Here are two pictures of the machine ready to make two different puddings. Draw what you think the puddings will look like when they are finished.

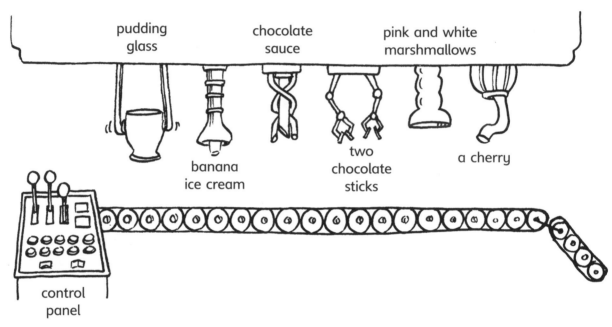

pudding glass

chocolate sauce

pink and white marshmallows

banana ice cream

two chocolate sticks

a cherry

control panel

cake base

dollop of cream

multi-coloured bean sweets

pink icing

nut chips

a fancy red bow

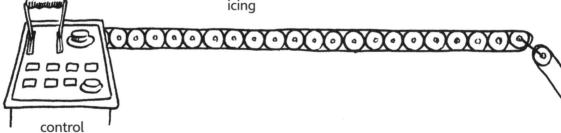

control panel

MORE TO DO!
- Draw the conveyer belt set up for another pudding and ask a friend to draw the finished pudding.
- Draw an enlarged picture of the control panel and think of all the things it could have on it!

MONSTER DRAWING RACE

Free Time Activities 7-9 © Molly Potter 2008

YOU WILL NEED:
- one set of monster fact cards per game
- scrap paper
- 2 pencils
- an even number of people – at least 4

(if there are four of you, you work as two teams of two.
If there are six of you then you work in two teams of three, etc.)

HOW TO WIN:
The aim of the game is to end up with more monster cards than your opposing team.

HOW TO PLAY:
- For each turn, there is one person who draws in each team (the drawer) and the rest of the team (which may only be one person) are guessers.
- Each member of each team takes it in turns to be the drawer.
- Spread the monster cards out on the table. The guessers turn away while one of the drawers points to one of the cards for both teams to draw at the same time (The teams can alternate who chooses but it makes no difference who chooses as all cards will be used in the end).
- The drawers then proceed to read the description and then draw the monster that they have chosen. (No letters, numbers, gestures or spoken words can be used by the drawers.)
- The first guess that anyone makes has to be accepted. The guess is made by picking up the correct fact card. If the guess is incorrect, then the other team wins that card.

This monster has three legs and only one eye with three tufts of hair sticking up above it.	This monster has really long hair and really long legs to match.	This monster can balance on the tip of a pencil but only with its three arms spread out.
This monster skips everywhere in its Wellington boots.	This monster insists on wearing a dotty tie.	This monster has warts all over its skin and toes shaped like carrots.
This monster has a habit of pouring custard all over its head then slipping over.	This monster is always scratching because of the fleas it has. It also has terrible dandruff.	This monster likes to wear flowers in its hair – especially daffodils.
This monster eats cars except for the tyres that it throws away.	This monster is always being sick, especially if it sees a tree.	This monster gets really angry every time it sees a car.
This monster throws stones at flowers because he thinks flowers are horrible.	This monster walks round in circles, gets dizzy and then falls off a cliff, every Saturday.	This monster has two large fangs that are often covered in bits of frog, because that is what it eats.

MORE TO DO!
Make up some monsters of your own to add to the game.

TREASURE ISLAND

See if you can work out where the two treasure chests are hidden and then make up some clues for another person.

TREASURE CHEST 1

I landed at the most southerly point of the island and rested for a while on a comfortable red seat and watched the sun rise. Sometime later, I walked along a cliff top until I found a shelter — but there was no one living there, so I could not ask for a cup of tea. Here I turned towards something spinning and walked towards it. I looked out to sea and could see a shipwreck. I turned and walked in the opposite direction to the shipwreck until I found a hill that looked as if it had a bit missing. Here I turned north and arrived at a beautiful tree just in time for my lunch. After lunch, I continued in the same direction until I arrived at a dark place that I did not dare go in to. At this point, I turned and walked into the wind, despite a really rather horrible smell. I soon saw where the smell was coming from and avoided it by taking a south westerly route. It was at the base of a prickly thing that I put the treasure.

TREASURE CHEST 2

1. The treasure is hidden in the eastern half of the island.
2. The treasure is exposed to the sky as it has no shelter of any kind nearby.
3. There are no trees near the treasure.
4. The treasure is not near anything that you can climb up.
5. The treasure is nowhere near anything wet or boggy.

Answer on p64

HUMAN NOISE BOX

You are going to create a human 'noise box'. You need to work with a partner. One of you is the controller who 'plays' the noise box and the other is the actual noise box but you can swap around at any time.

You need to come up with a variety of movements that you can do to make the noise box make a different sound. An obvious example is, if you pressed the noise box's nose it might make a whizz sound and it would do this every time. Another example is that if you wiggle its ear it might make a gurgling sound. Before you start, check that your noise box is happy to be touched!

See how many different noises you can make out of your noise box and decide if the noise is continuous or if it just happens once.

Some noises:
WHIZZ, GURGLE, BANG, CREAK, PING, BLOB BLOB BLOB, AN ENGINE NOISE, TWEET, A HUM, EEK, SQUEAK, AHHH, WOO, FFF, GLUG GLUG, BUZZ, CLUCK, MOO

Examples of things you can do to start the noises (remember the same noise always comes from each action):
press the nose, wiggle the ear, flick the knee, wiggle the fingers, lift the hair, run a finger along the eyebrow, poke the shoulder, turn the chin as if it were a knob, lightly pinch the cheek, tap on the foot, make the eye blink, rub the neck, pull the hair, lift a lip, move the foot, make the noise box sit, tilt its head, pull its nose, lower its chin, poke its belly button etc.

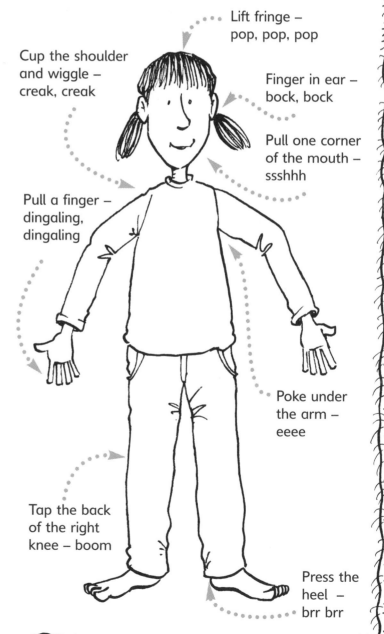

Lift fringe – pop, pop, pop

Cup the shoulder and wiggle – creak, creak

Finger in ear – bock, bock

Pull one corner of the mouth – ssshhh

Pull a finger – dingaling, dingaling

Poke under the arm – eeee

Tap the back of the right knee – boom

Press the heel – brr brr

Free Time Activities 7–9 © Molly Potter 2008

DOUBLE VISION

Find a friend to be your double. You and your double are going to practise doing some of the following things and then do them at exactly the same time and in exactly the same way. It will take a lot of practice and you might need a third person to tell you where something is not quite working. If you want to make it more difficult, work in threes and be triplets. This is bound to make you laugh!

PRACTISE:
- A funny walk
- A song with actions
- Getting up in the morning and cleaning your teeth
- A silly dance routine
- Welcoming someone into your house and offering them a cup of tea
- Receiving a phone call and being really excited about what someone is telling you
- Taking part in an obstacle race
- Having a snowball fight
- Having a tantrum
- Pretending to be an animal
- Itching all over
- Looking in the mirror and being confused by the face that you see
- Skipping using a skipping rope — messing up and treading on the rope!
- Daydreaming with your chin in your hand – with changing expressions on your face

THE AIM OLYMPICS

Can you think of lots of different ways that you could test how good someone is at aiming. These could be events in 'The Aim Olympics'.

HERE ARE SOME IDEAS TO GET YOU STARTED:

1. One person holds up a large hoop (as still as they can). The person being tested throws a ball or a bean bag through the hoop. Every time they manage to throw the object through the hoop, they take one step back so they are further away from the hoop and aim again. The first time that they do not get the object through the hoop, measure the distance between the person and the hoop. This is their 'score'. The bigger the distance the better the score.

2. Give a person five bean bags and ask them to try and get all five into a bucket placed a set distance away from them. Their score is how many they get in the bucket.

3. Flick a coin and try to get it in the centre of a target. The target could be 'scored' like this:

4. Use a netball ring and see how many times a person can get the ball in the ring if they are given five throws.

SOME MORE IDEAS
(you will have to make up the scoring)
- Throw small pieces of chalk at a target on an outside wall.
- Make a paper aeroplane and try to get it to land inside a hoop.
- Try to roll a marble so that it goes between two 'goal' posts.
- Try to bounce a ball inside two hoops that are a small distance apart. You need to get the ball in both hoops to score.
- Try to knock one or several home-made skittles over.
- Use a stick, like a hockey stick, to aim something into a goal.

OR SOME MORE UNUSUAL IDEAS
- Throw a teabag into a teapot!
- Throw a marshmallow into someone's mouth.
- Throw two sticks, one at a time, from a set distance and try and get them to land so they cross.
- Throw a freshly painted piece of sticky tack at a target on a piece of paper attached to the wall.

Free Time Activities 7-9 © Molly Potter 2008

HUNT THE PICTURE

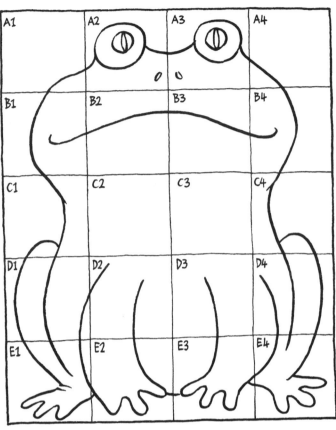

The grid (frog picture) cells:
A1, A2, A3, A4
B1, B2, B3, B4
C1, C2, C3, C4
D1, D2, D3, D4
E1, E2, E3, E4

NOTES FOR ADULTS

Cut this frog picture into the 20 squares and then stick/hide the squares in various places for the children to find. The children fill in the blank grid using what they have found in each rectangle. This will hopefully reproduce this picture of a frog!

	1	2	3	4
A				
B				
C				
D				
E				

ODD OBSTACLE COURSE

NOTES FOR ADULTS

This obstacle course is one with a difference because it is all about not touching obstacles. Depending on the equipment you have available, you need to lay out a course that depends on the skill of the person. Here are some examples of the kind of things you might like to include in your, 'Don't touch it' obstacle course.

Walk between the two skipping ropes without stepping on the paper.

Put your foot on a bean bag and manoeuvre it between the two ropes without touching the other bean bags or lifting your foot off the bean bag at any point.

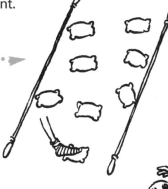

Walk between the two edge skipping ropes (or sticks) and do not touch the tangled skipping ropes (or ribbon).

Get through the gap between the chairs without touching the ropes.

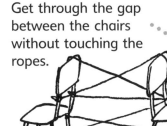

Bounce a ball inside each hoop without touching it.

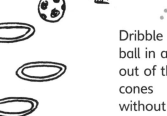

Dribble a ball in and out of the cones without touching them.

Crawl or walk through the dangling ribbon – attached to sticks (or skipping ropes) laid or tied across chairs or another piece of equipment.

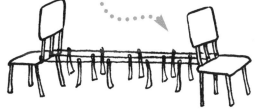

Walk between the benches (or a galley made with chairs) without a balloon touching you.

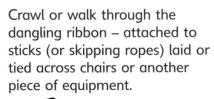

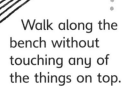

Walk along the bench without touching any of the things on top.

THINK ABOUT

- How you are going to score each person's attempt (timing, racing with another person – winner stays on).
- Whether you will give penalties for touching things or make participants start again.

- How you are going to check that a person has not touched anything (people watching).
- Whether or not you are going to have sections where people watching the 'race' deliberately try to touch the person – e.g. by throwing feathers at them.

Free Time Activities 7-9 © Molly Potter 2008

MIME IT

NOTES FOR ADULTS

Whisper one of the following things for someone to mime. Remind him/her to make the expression on his/her face look as if this was really happening. See if other people can guess what it is they are miming.

- You are walking along and a tiny black cloud is following you wherever you go and raining on your head.
- Your hair is growing at a rate of 1 cm every second.
- You walk along and tread in a huge blob of chewing gum that you end up getting tangled up in.
- You are blowing bubbles but all the bubbles fall straight to the floor with a thud.
- You put up an umbrella but discover that every time you do this, the rain falls from inside the umbrella.
- You are in a feather storm.
- You can smell the most delicious smell but cannot work out where it is coming from.
- Every time you take a step, you hear a painfully loud crashing sound.
- You see a two pound coin on the floor but every time you go to pick it up, it hops away.
- You are walking across a really hot floor.
- You have a walking stick but it starts to tickle you.
- A bird keeps swooping down and pecking you on the head.
- You have wellies on and you lose one welly in the mud and have to try and get it out without getting covered in mud – but fail miserably!
- You are lost. You keep seeing signs that you think will help you find your way but they get you even more lost.
- With each step that you take, your body gets heavier and heavier.
- Your feet are magnetic and attracted to each other toe to heel but repel each other when they are toe to toe.
- Your trousers keep falling down and your hat keeps blowing off your head.
- You stroke a dog and each time you do, it changes size.
- You have sticky tape wound round you several times – which makes it very hard to move!
- You are about to hit a ball with a bat but the bat appears to have a mind of its own.
- You are waiting in a queue that is moving forward slowly, but you are really impatient and keep knocking into the person in front of you.
- You are in a shop buying ten huge bags of potatoes.
- You are playing football but the ball keeps stopping dead – for no apparent reason.
- You are looking for a needle in a haystack.

Can the children make up some more things to mime?

BODY LANGUAGE

NOTES FOR ADULTS

1. Ask the children to make up signs and signals using their body, arms, hands and the expression on their faces to convey the following describing words but without using any sound whatsoever.

- Good
- Bad
- Lazy
- Tired
- Helpful
- Busy
- Excited
- Kind
- Naughty
- Fantastic
- Funny

- Happy
- Sad
- Beautiful
- Clever
- Hardworking
- Polite
- Patient
- Boring
- Weird
- Careful
- Honest

2. Now ask them to make up signs for these part sentences:

- Now, I am _____.

- The weather is _____.

- Today, I was _____.

- You are _____.

- I like _____people.

- I think school is_____.

3. Now see if they can 'say' whole sentences using what they have worked out for parts 1 and 2, e.g. Now I am busy.

4. Ask children to:
a) Practise the different ways they devised
for saying each thing.
b) Show what they have worked out to other people and see if
they can guess what is being said.
c) Demonstrate the signs and signals to other people as their friend
translates what is being said.

Free Time Activities 7-9 © Molly Potter 2008

SARIPPIA TRACK

This is Sarippia Track.

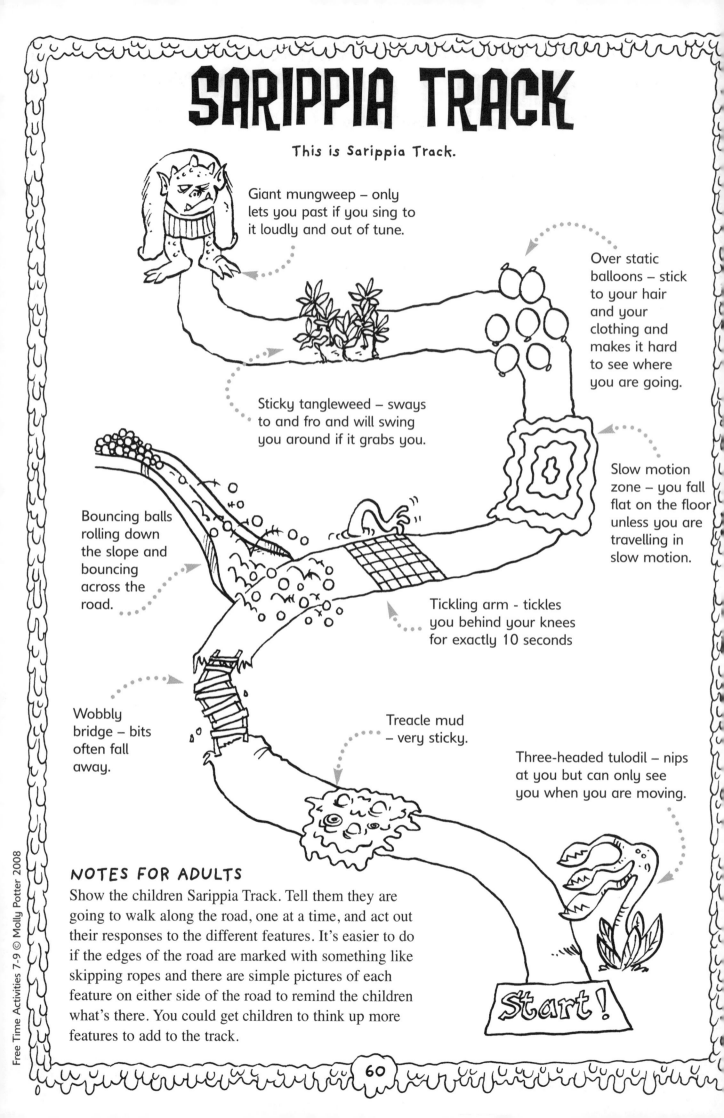

Giant mungweep – only lets you past if you sing to it loudly and out of tune.

Over static balloons – stick to your hair and your clothing and makes it hard to see where you are going.

Sticky tangleweed – sways to and fro and will swing you around if it grabs you.

Slow motion zone – you fall flat on the floor unless you are travelling in slow motion.

Bouncing balls rolling down the slope and bouncing across the road.

Tickling arm - tickles you behind your knees for exactly 10 seconds

Wobbly bridge – bits often fall away.

Treacle mud – very sticky.

Three-headed tulodil – nips at you but can only see you when you are moving.

NOTES FOR ADULTS

Show the children Sarippia Track. Tell them they are going to walk along the road, one at a time, and act out their responses to the different features. It's easier to do if the edges of the road are marked with something like skipping ropes and there are simple pictures of each feature on either side of the road to remind the children what's there. You could get children to think up more features to add to the track.

Start!

Free Time Activities 7-9 © Molly Potter 2008

MONSTER UGLY CONTEST

NOTES FOR ADULTS

Tell the children that you are having a Monster Ugly (not beauty) Contest. To do this everyone needs to draw the ugliest monster they can and enter it into the contest. The monster everyone votes as the ugliest will win!

Allow the children several attempts at drawing an ugly monster. Ask them to experiment with different features. Here are some to get them started.

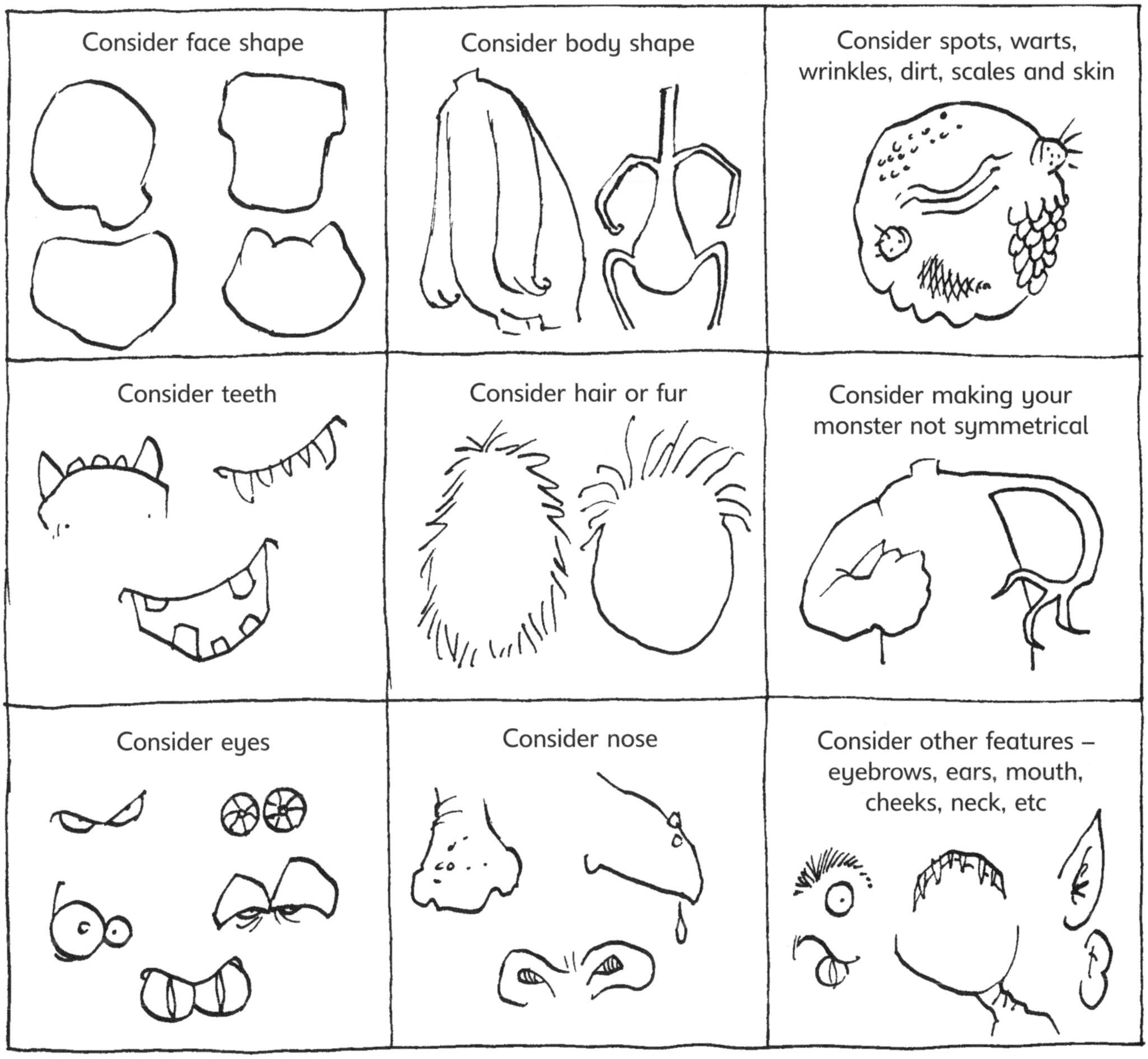

Consider face shape	Consider body shape	Consider spots, warts, wrinkles, dirt, scales and skin
Consider teeth	Consider hair or fur	Consider making your monster not symmetrical
Consider eyes	Consider nose	Consider other features – eyebrows, ears, mouth, cheeks, neck, etc

Ask children to give their monster a name and say where it comes from (e.g. Sog from Oppinia).
Children might like to make up some other details about their monsters:

• What it eats   • What job it has   • What it's scared of
• What it might say in response to the questions:

What, in your opinion, would make the world a better place? (e.g. smothering it in peanut butter)
What ambitions do you have? (e.g. get rid of all flowers and cute things)

Free Time Activities 7–9 © Molly Potter 2008

ANSWERS

LABEL PERSON (P13)

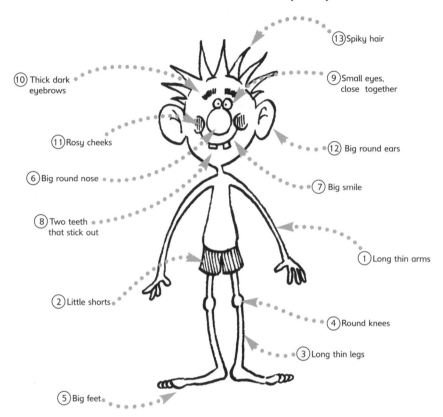

13 Spiky hair

10 Thick dark eyebrows

9 Small eyes, close together

11 Rosy cheeks

12 Big round ears

6 Big round nose

7 Big smile

8 Two teeth that stick out

1 Long thin arms

2 Little shorts

4 Round knees

3 Long thin legs

5 Big feet

CAMP SITE (P25)

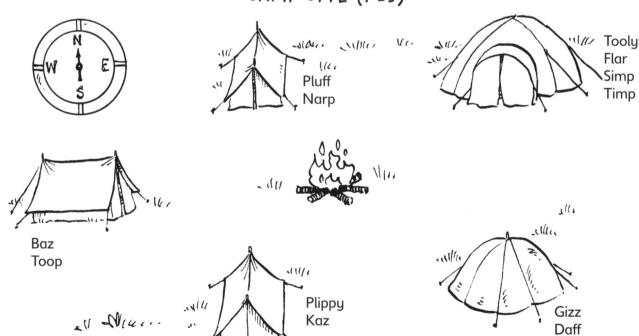

Pluff
Narp

Tooly
Flar
Simp
Timp

Baz
Toop

Plippy
Kaz

Gizz
Daff
Moop

WEIRD WORD HUNT (P43)

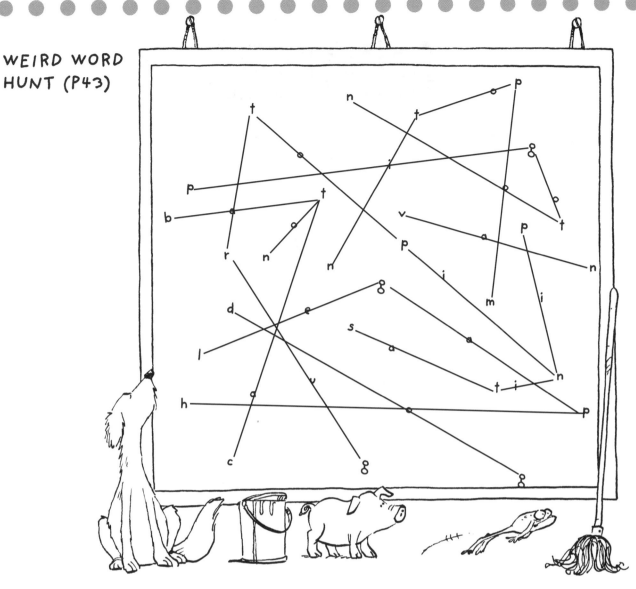

PLANET ZOOG (P46)

Parents are:

ZOOT & ZOG

Parents are:

ZAX & ZAG

Parents are:

ZAZ & ZOOT

Parents are:

ZOG & ZAX

Parents are:

ZIG & ZOG

Parents are:

ZAG & ZAZ

THE LONGEST LIST (P47)

Here are some example answers
- raisin, 5p, pin, pea, paper clip, etc
- aeroplane, house, bridge, sky, etc
- drive on the left, stop at red traffic lights, keep to the speed limit, not park on double yellow lines, stop at pedestrian crossings, not be drunk etc
- Little Bo Peep, Little Miss Muffet, Hey Diddle Diddle etc
- Baa, moo, cheep, meow, woof, neigh, tweet, etc
- banana, custard, mustard, marzipan, etc
- 14th Feb. – Valentine's Day, 5th November – Guy Fawkes 4th July – American Independence Day, 14th June – Bastille Day, 1st April – April Fools Day etc
- massive, enormous, tiny, minute, gigantic, etc
- Scramble, boil, fry, poach, pancakes, French bread etc
- hair, paper, wool, cotton, etc
- oil, alcohol, custard, milk, etc
- squash, cricket, netball, football, tennis, korfball, rounders etc
- washing machines, vacuum cleaners, lights, computers, dishwashers etc
- keys, coat hanger, candlestick, saucepan, gate, screw, needle, drain, padlock etc
- Y – why; U – you; 1 – won, one; NE – any; B4 – before; KT – Katy; NTT – entity; NEI - anyone

TREASURE ISLAND (P52)

1) Dusty cactus
2) Dotty soil

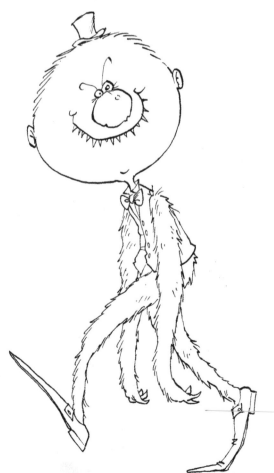